SUMMER

SEASONS OF THE YEAR

by
Harriet Brundle

SEASONS OF THE YEAR

©2016
Book Life
King's Lynn
Norfolk
PE30 4LS

ISBN: 978-1-910512-55-5

Written by:
Harriet Brundle

Edited by:
Gemma McMullen

Designed by:
Ian McMullen

A catalogue record for this book
is available from the British Library.

Contents

Words that appear like this can be found in the glossary on page 24.

Seasons of the Year

There are four seasons in a year. The seasons are called Spring, Summer, Autumn and Winter.

Each season is different. This book will tell you about Summer!

Summer

Summer comes after Spring and before Autumn.
The Summer months are June, July and August.

Summer

January

Sun	Mon	Tue	Wed	Thu	Fri	Sat
1	2	3	4	5	6	7
8	9	10	11	12	13	14
15	16	17	18	19	20	21
22	23	24	25	26	27	28
29	30	31				

February

Sun	Mon	Tue	Wed	Thu	Fri	Sat
			1	2	3	4
5	6	7	8	9	10	11
12	13	14	15	16	17	18
19	20	21	22	23	24	25
26	27	28	29			

March

Sun	Mon	Tue	Wed	Thu	Fri	Sat
			1	2	3
4	5	6	7	8	9	10
11	12	13	14	15	16	17
18	19	20	21	22	23	24
25	26	27	28	29	30	31

April

Sun	Mon	Tue	Wed	Thu	Fri	Sat
1	2	3	4	5	6	7
8	9	10	11	12	13	14
15	16	17	18	19	20	21
22	23	24	25	26	27	28
29	30					

May

Sun	Mon	Tue	Wed	Thu	Fri	Sat
	1	2	3	4	5
6	7	8	9	10	11	12
13	14	15	16	17	18	19
20	21	22	23	24	25	26
27	28	29	30	31		

June

Sun	Mon	Tue	Wed	Thu	Fri	Sat
					1	2
3	4	5	6	7	8	9
10	11	12	13	14	15	16
17	18	19	20	21	22	23
24	25	26	27	28	29	30

July

Sun	Mon	Tue	Wed	Thu	Fri	Sat
1	2	3	4	5	6	7
8	9	10	11	12	13	14
15	16	17	18	19	20	21
22	23	24	25	26	27	28
29	30	31				

August

Sun	Mon	Tue	Wed	Thu	Fri	Sat
		1	2	3	4
5	6	7	8	9	10	11
12	13	14	15	16	17	18
19	20	21	22	23	24	25
26	27	28	29	30	31	

September

Sun	Mon	Tue	Wed	Thu	Fri	Sat
						1
2	3	4	5	6	7	8
9	10	11	12	13	14	15
16	17	18	19	20	21	22
23	24	25	26	27	28	29
30						

October

Sun	Mon	Tue	Wed	Thu	Fri	Sat

November

Sun	Mon	Tue	Wed	Thu	Fri	Sat

December

Sun	Mon	Tue	Wed	Thu	Fri	Sat

In the Summertime, there are more hours of sunlight each day than in any other season.

The Weather

The sun shines in Summer. The weather feels warm and dry.

We must be careful in the sunshine not to burn our skin.

Don't forget your sun cream!

9

In the Garden

We can play in the garden when the weather is warm.

There are lots of insects in the garden in summer.

Which of these have you seen before?

Bee

Ant

Spider

Plants

Sunshine helps plants to grow. The flowers are colourful and the grass is green.

We must give the plants in the garden extra water in the Summertime because there is less rain.

Animals

Animals are growing in Summer. Some eat green grass so they can grow bigger.

Animals must eat plenty while there is lots of food. There is less food for them in the colder seasons.

Food

Lots of types of food grow in Summer. Apples and plums grow on the trees.

Apples

Plums

The fields are full of corn.
We use corn to make
breakfast cereals.

What do we Wear in Summer?

Hat

T-shirt

Shorts

In the Summertime we wear shorts and t-shirts because we want to stay cool.

Don't forget your hat to protect your head from the sun.

It is fun to go to the beach. We wear swimming costumes so we can go swimming.

Things to do in Summer

It is fun to go for a picnic in the sunshine.

What would you take in your picnic?

When the weather is sunny,
it is exciting to go to the park.

Fun in Summer

Draw a picture of something you enjoy doing in the Summertime.

It might be you eating an ice cream!

In places called deserts, the weather is sunny all year round.

Be careful not to look at the sun, even if you are wearing dark glasses. It will hurt your eyes!

23

Glossary

Index

Desert: a hot, sandy place with hardly any plants or animals.

Extra: more than usual.

Protect: to look after or cover.

Photo credits

Photocredits: Abbreviations: l-left, r-right, b-bottom, t-top, c-centre, m-middle. All images are courtesy of Shutterstock.com.
Front Cover, 5 – Sunny studio. 1 – vvvita. 2, 4lc – djgis. 3, 22bl – Andrey_Kuzmin. 4l Konstanttin. 4rc – Smileus. 4r – Triff. 6 – JonesHon. 7 – Zurijeta. 8 – BlueOrange Studio. 9 – mangostock. 10 – www.BillionPhotos.com. 11 – Serg64. 11bl,c – Evgeniy Ayupov. 11br – jps. 12 – Dudarev Mikhail. 13 – Subbotina Anna. 13tr – J. Marijs. 14 – Patrick Foto. 15 – Lucian Coman. 16 – gorillaimages 16inset – Valentyn Volkov. 17 – Sunny Forest. 17inset – Monkey Business Images. 18 – Olesia Bilkei. 19 – JaySi. 20 – iofoto. 21 – gpointstudio. 22r – Denphumi. 23bl – Ilya Andriyanov. 23inset – Mykola Mazuryk.